My Neighborhood:
The Words & Pictures of Inner-City Children

Compilation and narrative by
LINDA WALDMAN

Foreword by TIMOTHY GOODSELL
President, Hyde Park Bank,
and Hyde Park Bank Foundation

Afterword by JAMES B. COMER, MD
Maurice Falk Professor of Child Psychiatry
Yale Child Study Center

ISBN 0-9637517-0-0

To Elizabeth, and to all the children of
"My Neighborhood" whose honesty,
creativity and courage inspire us
to strive for a better world.

Hi my name is Bakari clay
an I'm going to tell you all
about my neigborhood. The
neiborhood that I live in
wasn't bad until about a year
ago. It use to be safe and clean
until they started to sell drugs,
and do drive bye's and
stick people up. I think
that people are so dumb for
killing each other over drugs,
coats, shoes, chains, and other
material items. Some days I'm
scared to even walk to school by
myself thinking that I'm gonna
get killed, kidnapped, or just plain
kicked around by some older
guys who wanna have a little
fun before school. Then there's even

your sister, dead. And if you have a child of your own, imagine the sounds of gunfire and screaming waking your child in the night.

Imagine being 6-year-old Sean Williams. Sean is afraid to go out of his house. "They shoot too much," he says. "They might shoot me. Maybe I should hide under my bed. Then I won't get shot."

Sean Williams is just one of the thousands of children living in the war zones across our country that we call inner-city neighborhoods. They are innocent children bereft of innocence. They are just as surely victims of atrocities as the children of Somalia and Bosnia. But they don't live halfway around the world; they live here, in our cities. They are the children of America, and they only want the right to which every American child is entitled. They want to be safe.

"We are not bad people, we are good people," says Lazinnia Wright, "so why do we have to live like this?" They are children of America, and they are telling us about the violence. They are telling us because they want us to make it stop. As Bakari Clay says, "I'm only 8 years old. I can't do it all by myself."

"MY NEIGHBORHOOD" CONTEST POSTER

Some of children's essays tell you about families who stay together and struggle to provide decent homes even in the middle of "hell." The fact these children can be creative and hopeful, and most miraculously, can smile and laugh in such an environment, can be attributed in great part to the strength of their families. "People say my area is the worst place on earth, but I'm surviving. I have a roof over my head, a bed to sleep on, a TV of my own and a nice family," writes Charlie Williams at the end of his essay. Most of all, the drawings and writings of these young people tell you that these kids are no different from any other children. They are "good kids" who like to play basketball, roller skate, go to the movies, and watch TV. They have dreams and plans. But through no fault of their own, they live in a world in which their worries and fears are those of people well beyond their age.

There are many children, however, who lack family structure and parental support. For them, it is the efforts of dedicated school principals and teachers that help them survive. Contrary to the popular perception of inner-city schools as corridors of chaos, where unsupervised and untaught children wreak havoc, many of the elementary schools attended by these children are havens of order. School is a lifeline for some of the children and the only place in which they feel safe.

The unfortunate truth, nonetheless, is that violence is robbing inner-city children of their right to an education. In *Children In Danger*, the authors write, "In order to deal with their fears of violence, the children employed defenses that were manifested as learning disabilities in the classroom. For poor children who already risk academic failure for cultural reasons, community violence is often scholastically the last straw." Whether it's through the traumatic effects of being a witness, or the inescapable fear of being a victim, violence interferes with a child's ability to learn. "I couldn't walk down the street without dodging bullets, I couldn't go to school because I couldn't," writes 9-year-old Donte Goodwin.

The situation has become even more devastating in recent years as violence has spread to the schoolyard. During the 1990-91 school year, Chicago police made 9,822 arrests on or near school grounds. The proliferation of guns has grown to such proportions that 13-year-olds shoot at each other on the playground. That should be unthinkable in a civilized society.

As you read the pages that follow, remember that these children were not asked to describe violence; they were asked to describe their neighborhoods. Then, take a moment and remember what it was like to be 6 years old. Remember who and what you knew, and the games you played. Remember your playground and neighborhood, and how safe you felt there. Remember guns that only shot water.

Then, imagine that same 6-year-old, and imagine that the guns are the kind that kill, and they might kill you. Imagine that your playground is a slab of concrete covered with broken glass and broken needles. Imagine that when a car drives by you're afraid it could leave you, or your neighbor, or

While almost every written entry reflects the violence they see, some of the children seemed able to escape their surroundings, and to be imaginative in their drawings. Many of the children drew the kinds of images they might see in books - sunny skies, traditional houses, dogs, cars, and apple trees.

But many of the drawings are deceptively innocent. In the colorful pictures of buildings and trees and kids playing, one might see, on closer examination, people shooting each other, or a drug deal occurring, or a police car. Seven-year-old Lakina Lollar drew a picture of the projects where she lives. There are two bright yellow suns, some blue clouds, and a playground with smiling people, one of whom is shooting a gun. Above them, Lakina has printed the words, "Please stop the shooting. We can't play."

With few exceptions, the entries offer graphic portrayals of a world that few of us could imagine, let alone survive. "We cry we weep, we can't go outside and play, because our parents believe, that we will be killed that day," reads a poem by 11-year-old Cynthia Chambers.

Cynthia's parents' fears are not unfounded. In 1992, according to the *Chicago Sun Times*, the police department recorded 915 murders in Chicago, 70% of which were committed with handguns. In that year alone, Chicago police confiscated 18,500 handguns. In *Children In Danger*, (San Francisco: Jossey-Bass Publishers, 1992), authors Garbarino, Dubrow, Kostelny, and Pardo document the toll violence takes on the children of the inner city, and conclude that by the time they've reached five years of age, the majority of these children have had encounters with shootings.

As they get older, many inner-city children have to physically fight to stay out of gangs. The future is so uncertain for these kids, birthdays are often noted not by the phrase, "He turned 10," but by, "He made 10."

Cynthia, Charlie, Demetrius, Carolyn, Alexis, Lakina and all the others have witnessed more violence in their few years than most people will in the entire span of their lives. The remarkable thing about these children, however, is that they have not given up. To find only despair and devastation in their words and pictures is to do them a great disservice. One finds wonderful creativity, energy and talent here, as well. These inner-city children speak with great eloquence. Their words and pictures tell you about much more than the desperate conditions of their neighborhoods; they speak about courage and hope. They tell you about children who still believe in the future. "I believe in God," says 8-year-old Gail Whitmore, "and I know one day we will be in a gooder place."

---

v

Preface

● ● ●

"HELLO, MY NAME IS CHARLIE WILLIAMS...I LIVE IN A SLUM. SOME PEOPLE CALL IT A HELL ON EARTH AND SO DO I." Charlie Williams is 12 years old, and that's how he describes his neighborhood. Charlie does not live in Bosnia or Beirut or Somalia; he lives in Chicago. Charlie's neighborhood is one of the dozens of communities in the backyards of our cities that we see or hear about only when there is an incident of violence. But violence is not incidental in these neighborhoods. It is an ever present reality that lies in wait each time a door is opened. It hangs in the dark corners of the hallways, hovers over the playgrounds, and strikes out from the windows of passing cars. It violates the innocence of childhood. "I'm only in third grade," says 9-year-old Alexis Williams, "and I know lots of bad things that people shouldn't do."

How Charlie and Alexis came to describe their neighborhoods in such a way reveals the extent to which violence has permeated their consciousness . These kids merely entered a contest, one which was intended to elicit expressions of community pride. In October of 1992, Hyde Park Bank of Chicago sponsored a contest for elementary school children from the areas around the bank, some of which are among the most economically depressed communities in the country.

Hundreds of students from 53 schools entered Hyde Park Bank's contest. The entries came in many forms. Some of the essays were neatly typed, others were handwritten. While a few of the children from the middle-class pockets near the bank described nice, peaceful neighborhoods, the great majority told a different story. They described places where crime, anger and fear destroy any sense of neighborhood pride. It is hard to be proud of where you live, when you think you live in "hell." "My neighborhood is like a hell hole," writes Carolyn Bradley. Carolyn is 10 years old and she says sometimes she cries because she wants to live somewhere else.

The words the children wrote and the pictures they drew are profound and moving, and all the more compelling because they come from children. This is not an outsider's view. This is not media coverage. This is devastation and violence as described firsthand by children who experience it every day. You may forget the story on the 10 o'clock news, but you will not forget the words or images of these young people. "Leaving for school is scary. You never know when you might get shot. You never know when someone might shoot at you out of a window," writes 13-year-old Demetrius Jones. He titled his essay "Living One Day At A Time."

Foreword

BY TIMOTHY GOODSELL
President, Hyde Park Bank, & Hyde Park Bank Foundation

● ● ●

THE "MY NEIGHBORHOOD" CONTEST STARTED AS A MARKETING IDEA. Hyde Park Bank wanted to produce a brochure describing our community reinvestment efforts. One of the designs presented to us featured children's drawings. We liked this idea because it focused on children as the heart and future of the community. Also, sponsoring a contest to obtain the words and pictures needed for the brochure gave us the opportunity to become involved with the schools in the area. To announce the contest, we used a fun and lighthearted poster which was displayed in school corridors. We anticipated that the tone of the entries would be the same as that of the poster. We thought we would have brightly colored, childish drawings of trees and houses, and funny little stories about the postman and the people on the block. The responses we received stunned us.

Our misapprehension became clear with the very first entry we read. It belonged to 8-year-old Gail Whitmore. Upon reading the first sentence of Gail's essay, our original intentions were overshadowed by much larger, more imperative issues. "In my neighborhood there is a lot of shooting and three people got shot," Gail began. Throughout the judging process, as we read and reviewed hundreds of essays and drawings describing relentless violence and deplorable conditions, our emotions ran from indignation, to outrage, to despair. Many times we were moved to tears, but more importantly we were moved, and by the time the judging was over we were committed to bringing the power of these words and pictures to a larger audience. We hoped to help others learn, as we had learned, that violence is robbing thousands of innocent children of their civil rights. Because of violence, these children cannot play or learn or even sleep without fear.

Through the publication of the *My Neighborhood* book, we are hopeful that the problems of our communities and others like them will be taken to heart by people of all communities. We believe that awareness can lead to caring, and caring to action. And if enough action is taken, one day, when they are asked to describe their neighborhoods, the children of the inner city will answer with childish descriptions of peaceful playgrounds and friendly neighbors.

I am Black

I am beautiful

My speech is clear

My mind is focused

See me

Know me

I am a child of the universe

Reprinted by permission of the Florence B. Price School

more fear when walking home
because face it I live a block
away from school but in this world
we live in today that's a long walk home anything
could happen. But I just
take a deep breath and keep
my head to the sky hoping that
the police or someone can make
my neiborhood safe to live in
again Someday. There's trouble
anywhere you go so I'm gonna do
all I can to help my neiborhood
be the cleanest and safest
place I can but I'm only 8 years
old I can't do it all by myself.
When I grow older I'm gonna be
the best I can be so I can make
a difference some day.

My Neighborhood

My neighborhood
is so bad. They shoot
people. I hate when
they be shot. They shoot
to much. They die.
And they do drugs.
I see houses with
gates. they keep people
From coming in.

TRAPPED IN MY HOUSE

The houses in my neighborhood look so pretty, but I don't see my neighborhood much. I only go outside when I get in the car or go to school. I don't like my neighborhood, because they shoot too much. They might shoot me. So, I stay in the house. I think it's safe there. One time, some bullets hit our window. I was afraid. My house doesn't seem safe anymore. Maybe, I should hide under my bed. Then I won't get shot.

My dog is missing. He use to play with the other dogs. He use to look after my house. Maybe they shot him. Maybe they shot him so they can rob my house.

My neighborhood is getting worse. On Halloween, a man snatched my money out of my hand and started running. I didn't like that. He didn't have to steal my money. What will he do with it? My mother said he will buy drugs. Why do they do drugs? I don't know why. Maybe, because they want to die. I see the police a lot. The police want them in jail so they wont steal anymore.

Maybe, everyone should just move.

SEAN NEVER DID FIND HIS DOG, SCRAPS. Although Scraps was just a mutt, Sean looked for him first thing each day when he came home from school. "One day," Sean says, "he wasn't there."

The shooting continues around Sean's house. Recently, a bullet went through the radiator of the family car. Sean's father keeps the window blinds closed so they don't see the violence. Inside the house, Sean plays with his video games and reads books - *Cinderella* and *Henny Penny* are two of his favorites.

Every night Sean and his dad play a reading game. "I'll tell Sean my eyes are old and bad and he needs to read things for me," says Richard Williams. "We'll read out of the bible or the newspaper, and from that I'll find out what he knows and what he has trouble with. Then we work on it. Then he reads his homework out loud, more than once, so he can get it right."

SEAN WILLIAMS

Sean says he wants to be a fireman when he grows up, but unlike most kids his age, he already has some experience. He is a regular visitor at the nearby fire station where his father's friend is captain, and has been given an honorary engine.

When he's not afraid to go outside, Sean's favorite outdoor activities are riding his skateboard and playing baseball. He also likes to ride in the car. "He never closes his eyes in the car," says Sean's dad. "He wants to see everything. He's just an all-American boy to me."

CAMERON TODD - AGE 7

I wish I could fix every thing up and if I could it wouldn't be so bad now.

I do wish people wouldn't burn down our homes and shoot down our neighbors because if you have a right to live we do to.

Those who are doing drugs if you can help it please quit it because it's bad for you and it will also kill you. If don't know that you should.

I'm only in third grade and I know lots of bad things that people shouldn't do. Our neighborhood needs to look like other states and countries. It is not good to shoot and rob and kill other people not even policemen because if you get caught it is not any ones ells problem.

I want to get together with someone who knows what they are doing and fix this place up. You shouldn't have to live in garbge and filth you have a right to live in a clean neighborhood. To.

ALEXIS WILLIAMS · AGE 9

ALEXIS DOES INDEED KNOW "LOTS OF bad things that people shouldn't do." She knows that people urinate on her building. She'd like to build a fence to keep them away. And she knows that she must be watchful when she goes to the grocery store, because she might get shot. In fact, one day when she was outside playing with a friend, the shooting began and she had to run home. Now when she hears shots, she starts shivering. "Sometimes," she says, "I think it's fireworks."

Still, Alexis finds ways to be happy. She is happy about the people in her neighborhood who know her and watch out for her. And she is happy when she is with her mother. "Me and my mother go skating together - sometimes just me and her," she says. "Sometimes we go to the park and play on the swings and read books. And we like to race. My mother ran track and can run real fast and good. She can skate good, too. She taught me. And she's gonna teach me how to ice skate."

ALEXIS WILLIAMS

With a 20-year-old sister away at college, Alexis is the oldest child at home. As such, she helps her mother take care of her two little sisters. She also assists with the cooking and shopping - all responsibilities she says she enjoys, because they show her mother trusts her.

An honor roll student earning A's and B's, Alexis would like to be a doctor when she grows up, "so I can help my family and other good people," she says. Right now, Alexis is saving her allowance to buy things for the house. "There's some things we don't have," she says. "I'd like to buy an apron for my mother and some knobs for the cabinets."

MARCUS LEE - AGE 8

1 3

I hope for a better Neighborhood.

There are a lot of good things and bad things in my neighborhood. The bad things are. There is a lot of gang violence where I live. People are getting shot this happens a lot in the summer. They fight a lot where I live. people are getting hurt a lot where I live. That makes me fill sad to know that people can't get along with each other, in my neighborhood. I am angry because me and my little sisters can't go out side and play or ride our bicycles. The good things in my neighborhood are. The buildings where I live have been locked down. That makes us a little safer. The other good thing are, people took time to plant baby trees, grass, flowers, and bushes. Because before all we had was dirt and mud. I fill happy because people care enuafe to come here and help make the neighborhood look better. It shows that some people care. It gives me hope, And there is not a lot of hope where I live. But as long as I have hope that we can change our Neighborhood maybe the gangs and the drugs will just go away. And the little beauty that I see might grow into a big beauitful Neighborhood.

SHANDEN THEDFORD - AGE 8

SHANDEN HAS A PET FISH NAMED LEONA Helmsley. When Mrs. Helmsley was in the news, Shanden felt bad that everyone was picking on her, so he named his fish after her. "He's a builder and a dreamer," says Shanden's mother of her son. He likes to construct walls, buildings, and cars, and he'll use just about anything in his construction - bottle caps, toilet paper rolls, legos. An honor student, he also likes to read and practice his cornet, which he plays in beginner band in school.

SHANDEN THEDFORD AND SISTER, KENNICE

As summer approaches, Shanden is fearful about going outside not only for himself but for his two younger sisters, as well. As the oldest child and only boy, Shanden feels responsible for the girls, ages 6 and 2. "There be a lot of fighting - mostly in the summer. They be shooting and everybody jump down," he says. There are times, though, when the children do play outside. These are the times they go to the lake with their mother and father. There, they feel safe riding their bikes.

Shanden's mother, Shanda, watches her children very closely. Each day she walks them to and from school where she is a volunteer. She says she would like to move her family someplace safer. Shanda says if she lives to get out of the projects, she's going to write a book called "Caught In The Crossfire." But she wants people to know that there are decent people living in the projects as well. "There is an element of badness, but there are good people here too. As long as we instill values in our kids, they'll grow up okay," says Shanda. "Not everyone here is bad. I'd like people to know that."

Most of the lights are out in the stairway leading up to Justin's fourth floor apartment. Gang symbols and graffiti cover the walls. But at the top of the stairs, the landing is neat and clean, and on the doorway there's a carved wooden sign that reads, "The Myles Family." Inside, seven of the nine children, one grandchild and Mr. and Mrs. Myles are at home. One daughter is at Northern Illinois University. Another is living elsewhere.

Mrs. Myles comments several times on how amazed she is that anyone would come to their home. "Weren't you afraid to come here?" she asks. She says the building used to be known as the "drug building," and it was not uncommon to find needles and condoms in the stairwells. "But," she says, "it has gotten better lately."

JUSTIN MYLES & FAMILY

The family is open and affable, laughing, teasing, and generally enjoying each other. Justin seems to be the quiet one, but his mother explains he's only shy around strangers. She describes him as curious and very energetic. "He takes up for people - defends other kids," she says, "and he loves to sing in church. He has a beautiful voice." Justin's mother is grateful that her children get along well together. "I pray for them to stay out of trouble," she says. Because she doesn't like the kids to play outside, she buys toys and games at local thrift stores to occupy them inside the house. One of her purchases is an easel for Justin. When it is brought into the room, Justin seems happy and more comfortable in front of his pad of paper than he is in the spotlight. It is not surprising that his favorite class at school is art. He also likes to read and play basketball. His mother says he does very well in school and he has been on the honor roll, "but it's hard to get him to do his homework."

Mrs. Myles would like to find a better place to live, but says it's difficult with so large a family. She is also unsure of where to go. "Some neighborhoods may look better," she says, "but what's happening here is spreading everywhere."

My Neighborhood

My Neighborhood is bad. They be smoking. I don't like that. You will die.
They call Themselves Gangster. I Live on 48 st that where they be gangbang at.
They be shooting people and they be shooting dice, my friend do it to.

VINCENT WINSTON - AGE 7

19

My neighborhood is a neighborhood that is filled with lead things. I live in a tall white project building. There are lots and lots of people here. Most of these people are grown-ups and some are small kids like me. It is always very crowded in my building and there is always a lot of noise here. It is sometimes hard for small people like me to go and play with my friends, because of all the bad things here. Some of the bad things are grown-ups fussing with each other. They always seem to be mad at each other. There is always some kind of confusion in my building. It is not very safe in my building. You have to be careful when you come into the building because you might

LAZINNIA WRIGHT - AGE 9

get shot by someone who is trying to shoot someone else. That happens all the time. People begin to run and scream when the shooting begins. It is almost like living in a War movie. The bad guys against the good guys. The building is never clean, we have to walk through a lot of garbage just to get to our house. The walls are dark and dingy in the hallways. and it is very scary. We have to wait a long time to get on the elevators when they are working. When the elevators are not working we have to walk up a lot of stairs to reach the 7th floor. When I look out the window there are still bad things to see. There are people walking around. Policeman and police cars sirens going off

LAZINNIA WRIGHT · AGE 9

all the time. There are liquor stores where people stand out side and beg for money. There are prostitutes who stand out side even when it is cold outside. There are drug dealers outside who are selling drugs to anyone that will buy them even little kids like me. The way I feel about my neighborhood is, it not a very good place to live. I wish sometimes that my mother, my sister, my brother and me did not have to live in this neighborhood. We are not bad people, we are good people, so why do we have to live like this. We have to walk through a neighborhood that is filled with empty lots, empty buildings and people just do not care. We want a better place to live and grow.

On Saturdays Lazinnia likes to visit her grandmother, not only because she enjoys her company, but because she and her mother often stop by a nearby arcade. There her mother wins stuffed animals for Lazinnia. The collection of furry creatures covering Lazinnia's bed is a drastic contrast to the chaos and fear in the project where she lives. In the comfort of her apartment, Lazinnia seems to feel relatively safe with an older brother and sister, and "a mother who takes care of me." In fact, Lazinnia strives to be like her older siblings. They both have won basketball trophies and she is trying to get on the basketball team in her school.

Lazinnia is serious about her school work. A straight A student, she has been on the honor roll every semester. She loves to read and goes to a reading class every morning at 7:30. Frequently Lazinnia comes home from school with a new book, which she excitedly describes to her mother. Lazinnia also likes math and social studies and wants to be a teacher so she can teach those subjects to other children. "If they would stop the shooting and killing," says Lazinnia, "and people would stay in school instead of on the streets, the world would be a better place."

LAZINNIA WRIGHT

In my neighborhood there is a lot of shooting and three people got shot. On the next day when I was going to school I saw a little stream of blood on the ground. One day after school me and my mother had to dodge bullets I was not scared. There is a church and a school that I go to in my neighborhood. There are a lot of stores in my neighborhood also. There are robbers that live in my building, they broke into our house twice. There are rowhouses in my neighborhood and a man got shot, and he was dead. On another day I saw a boy named Zak get shot by J&B. By King High School Susan Harris got shot and she died. It was in the newspaper. When me and my mother was going to church we could see the fire from the guns being shot in 4414 building. I was not scared. In my neighborhood there are to many fights. I have never been in a fight before. There are many trees in my neighborhood. God is going to come back one day and judge the whole world. Not just my neighborhood. I know these are really really bad things, but I have some good things in my neighborhood. Like sometimes my neighborhood is peaceful and quiet and there is no shooting. When me and my mother and some of my friends go to the lake we have a lot of fun. Sometimes the children in my building go to Sunday School with me and my mother. Also the building I live in is so tall I can see downtown and the lake. It looks so pretty. I believe in God and I know one day we will be in a gooder place than we are now.

THE END

ALTHOUGH GAIL'S RESIDENCE IS THE housing project directly across the street from her school, through books she has lived in other more magical places. Last year Gail read 100 books and did reports on every one of them. She also had perfect attendance and earned straight A's. She is a member of her school's Great Books Club and designates biographies and "long books" as those she enjoys most. She'd like to be a teacher and an author of fairy tales, and says her favorite fairy tale is *Beauty and the Beast*.

The joy of reading runs in Gail's family. Her mother, Sharon, confesses she reads everything she can get her hands on. A member of the local school council and a daily volunteer at the school, Sharon is completely devoted to Gail, who is her only child. "It's just me and her," says Sharon. "We do everything together. If I'm invited somewhere, and she can't go, most times I don't go."

Sharon works hard to protect Gail from the violence, not just physically but psychologically, as well. While Gail has heard the shooting and seen the effects of it - there is a gang rivalry between the residents of her building and the one across the way - she has not translated that to personal fear. "Gail's not old enough yet to be afraid. When you're young you think you're gonna be here a long time," explains Sharon. "So I monitor her and let her keep her freedom, 'cause once you rob that from a child, you can't never get it back."

GAIL WHITMORE & HER MOTHER

State way

Bus

My neighborhood is the middle of a danger zone. It's dark, dirty and deserted. Sometimes the street lights doesn't work. There are people who won't put their trash in cans. I've seen people in cars stop, dump trash on the curb sides. My neighborhood has vacants lots and abandon buildings. A few yards have grass. Most lots are covered by weeds and garbage.

When I pass those buildings I feel scared. It seems someone's watching me. I've seen people inside those buildings, some hanging around, the others are homeless. I'm very thankful I have a home, food to eat and a family who loves me. People hangout in our hallway. Last month they stole our mail. The landlord put new locks on both doors. Mom says never talk to strangers,never take money from anyone and never get into a strangers car. If I do,someone might hurt me real bad.

We have many businesses in our neighborhood. There are several food stores,several restaurants,several beauty shops and a barber school. Several medical and dental offices, two cleaners, a pawn shop, a record shop, five taverns, two newspaper stands, a pool hall, a used furniture store and one where Woolworth's use to be.

My brother and I stay in the house alot. When we go outside kids pick at us. Mom says there's more to life than the streets. We're only allowed to go to the store before dark.

JULIAN FREEMAN - AGE 9

In our building there's the basement, Ms Bobbie, Ms Adie and and Mr and Mrs Ed. Ms.Bobbie died. The neighbors said she drank herself to death. Ms. Adie recently had a stroke, she's in a wheelchair. She's moving so she can get help. Mr. Ed loves to fish. He caught a huge fish, it was hanging from a tree in the backyard. I have never seen a fish this big. My mom said they're going to cut it, cook it and eat it.

On the first floor, Mr and Mrs Cumberlander. Next door Ms. Rose who stays to herself. On the second floor, Ms.Thelma, her son John's mother-in-law. Next door there's the Stewart's. Since John's mother-in-law died, they've had two other roommmates. Felix and now anew one. On the third floor there's my mom , my brother and her boyfriend. Next door are the Nick brothers and Ed's brother Fred. My brother and I are the only children in the building. The landlord doesn't want children. Most of the children who have lived here have brokwn windows, messed up walls and set fires.

I pray that we'll move into a beautiful house. My brother and I will have a backyard with a swimming pool. The neighborhood will be beautiful. There'll be trees, grass and a playground. There won't be any drugs, gangs or abandon buildings. One day my dream will come true. And I'll be free from the boys in the hood.

ALTHOUGH HE'S THE QUIETER, MORE peaceful brother, Julian occasionally finds himself fighting to defend his younger sibling, Todd. "Todd likes to play rough," explains their mother, "and then Julian has to step in for him. He's always there for him." Julian admits that he worries a little bit about his younger brother and protects him. "If somebody hit him, I be stopping them," he says. "I be walking him home from school every day, watching out for him."

Just two years apart, the brothers are best friends. Together they play football, basketball, ride bikes, and watch TV. Julian is particularly fond of Ninja turtles. He also likes magazines of all kinds - "zillions," says his mother.

JULIAN FREEMAN (RIGHT) AND BROTHER, TODD

Julian enjoys being outside, but says he doesn't always feel safe there. "Somebody might be in a car shooting, and they might shoot me or my brother," he says. His mother says Julian worries about the gangs and will cross the street if he sees them coming. "He knows they mean trouble. He's a peaceful boy," she says. "He doesn't like fighting."

Sun

Lakina Lollar AGE 7.

We can't
Play

Please
Stop The Shooting

LAKINA SITS PRETTILY ON HER FRILLY, PINK-CANOPIED BED, AND DESCRIBES her drawing: "There's a man shooting at another grownup on the playground, and there's little kids playing there and the kids is trying to get out of the playground, but they can't 'cause they're in the middle, so they have to lie on the ground." Seeing Lakina in her neat little room, it is hard to imagine the graffiti on the walls right outside the door of her project apartment, or the violence that is a daily threat on the playground below. Lakina says there's a lot of shooting. She sees it from her apartment, and when it starts she goes under the covers in her mother's room.

Lakina likes to skate, play 7-up, and hide-and-seek, but she has to be content with riding her bike and skating on the breezeway outside her apartment. "My mother don't let me down there (on the playground), 'cause they shoot down there," she says. "And ain't nothing to play with anyway. There's no swings and the slide is all messed up and the monkey bar is cut off."

The youngest of three children, Lakina has two brothers, aged 13 and 18. The oldest brother is on the honor roll at his high school and helps Lakina with her homework. He says she works hard at school. "School is important to the whole family," explains Lakina's mother. "It's the only way to be productive in today's society." Lakina would like to be a lawyer when she grows up because, "I want to help people and stop them from fighting." For now, Lakina says she'd just like to get out of the projects.

LAKINA LOLLAR

I do not like my Neighborhood it is not Safe. I am scared to go to the store because they be shooting and killing people and rapping people and I do not want to get killed because I want to finish school and get a Job and have my own family one day, I love lots of   people and they love me to I am scared of the gangbangers because there are a lot of people getting killed or murdered and, I do not like when people are dead because I like to meet more people so that we can be come friends I love people.

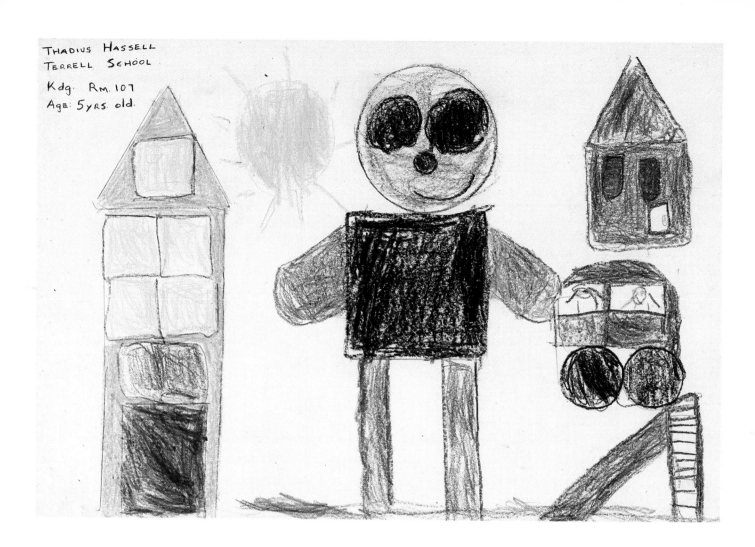

THADIUS HASSELL TERRELL SCHOOL

Kdg. Rm. 107
Age: 5yrs. old.

THADIUS HASSELL - AGE 5
34

THADIUS SPEAKS SO SOFTLY THAT one has to lean in very close to hear him. Then he tells you that he'd like to be a Ninja turtle (specifically Leo) so he can play in the sewers. After school Thadius comes straight home to do his homework and play with his four brothers and one sister. Together they watch Batman, or sometimes they draw.

As Thadius stands by the window, his big, sad eyes resemble those in the self-portrait he did for the "My Neighborhood" contest. Thadius says he entered the contest because he wanted to draw a picture. At school, Thadius enjoys building things with blocks - "things," he says, "like motorcycles and buildings and jails."

THADIUS HASSELL

The street where I Live, is big and wide.
you have to be very careful, if you come outside,
There are people, Cars and all Kinds of sounds
When you're crossing the street, always look around.

There are grocery stores, laundermats and a shopping mall
There are trains and buildings some are 4 stories tall
There's our school, a beauty shop and a ice cream store,
game rooms, meat markets and lots lots more.

Some times theres crime, on the street at night
They argue, drink cuss and fight,
As I sit in the window, theres a siren not far
When I look out again I see a police caR.

I try to be careful, when Im all alone
Like going to school, and coming home.
I look all around me and hear sounds far away,
But this is my ~~~~~~~~~
          neighborhood, and I face it everyday.

CIARA NEEALY · AGE 9

anthony Lowe
Burke school Room 212
grade 2

My Neighbor
hood

I dont want any body
to go out side
because they
are getting shot.
we live in a kind of Big house
I see grown people
and kids around my
house.

My neighborhood is
some time it is bad
around my house and
some times it is
not bad around
my house. they
shoot people

and they die.

I use to love my neighborhood,
I use to think it was a great
place, until I woke up one day
and there the Nightmare Stared me in
the face.

The drugs the gangs and the
killing.
made me have this feeling, not of
hope, not of love, but of hate.

I couldn't walk down the steet
with out ducking from bullets
I couldn't go to School because
I couldn't

But I won't put up with this
for long, because this is my
neighborhood this is my home!

DONTE GOODWIN - AGE 10

For years Donte was the baby of the family and enjoyed the attention he got from his mother, brother, and sister. But with the births of two younger brothers Donte became a child in the middle, not close in age to any of his siblings. Perhaps that is why he seems surprised by all the attention focused on him now.

Shy and quiet around strangers, Donte does not smile easily. But when it's time to take his picture, he tilts his head back, his eyebrows go up slightly and one can almost detect the look of pleasure on his face. When coaxed, he proudly points to a story he wrote displayed on the school bulletin board.

This achievement is evidence of a recent turnaround for Donte. His mother thinks that his improvements in school have been prompted in part by the award he received in the "My Neighborhood" contest. "After the births of his younger brothers," she says, "Donte's school work fell off. But the recognition he has received lately, changed his life."

DONTE GOODWIN

With new interest in reading and writing, Donte's work has improved, and last month he was named student of the month. He likes to write, and he thinks that writing will help him when he's a preacher like Rev. Martin at his church. Right now, though, Donte is preoccupied with collecting baseball cards. Because he is small for his age, Donte's mother would rather keep him inside. "They pick on him and try to get him in gangs," she says. "But they don't bring them in my home. I don't let gangs in here. I tell Donte, if you ain't worked for no money, you ain't got no money." Asked to talk about his award-winning poem, Donte says, "I'd like to stop the shooting, selling drugs, killing and beating up people. I'd like someone to think up ideas to do that."

JARTHUR WILLIAMS - AGE 14

42

Killings-Gangs- Stealing - Drugs - Graffiti

These (are) the things in my neighborhood I see,
It doesn't seem like I am free.

We cry (we) weep, WE can't go outside (and) play,
because (our) Parents believe, that we will be
Killed that day.

I wish I (had) a big vacuum cleaner, (to) wipe
out all the Killings, and drugs, I also want
the vacuum cleaner to wipe out all the thugs.

It's hard to talk about my neighborhood with
all the guns, gangs, (and) drug dealings,
because of (the) death and because of the
tears, PLEASE for us children, "STOP
THE KILLINGS!"

CYNTHIA CHAMBERS - AGE 11

JASMINE BROWNING - AGE 13

44

ACCORDING TO HER ART TEACHER, JASMINE HAS AN INDOMITABLE SPIRIT. WHEN JASMINE was eight years old, her mother died of what Jasmine says was a drug overdose. She then spent a period of time in foster homes - a time, she says, that was very scary. Now Jasmine lives with her father. Her 8-year-old sister lives "somewhere else," she says.

Jasmine and her father's home is quite a distance from the school she attends, but because the school is where she has always gone, and where her friends are, he drives her there every morning. Still, all is not easy for Jasmine at this predominantly African-American school. Because she is of mixed race and has a fair complexion, Jasmine faces her own challenges. "Some kids mess with me because I'm light-skinned and have longer hair," she says. "I think they're jealous. I don't see why they're jealous. They should be happy with what they have."

Despite all she has experienced, Jasmine succeeds. She has many friends, and is an avid fan of the music group TLC - the one fact about herself that she would like everyone to know. She also earns good grades, and has definite plans for the future. "I want to go to Notre Dame and be a gymnastics teacher," she says. She wants to teach gymnastics because she likes working with little children. In fact, she spends most days after school with her nieces and nephews - aged 3 to 5. Together they play school with Jasmine as the teacher, instructing her pupils in writing, reading, and coloring.

Photo by Patricia Evans

JASMINE BROWNING

Jasmine is concerned about children, and says if she could do anything to make the world a better place, she would, "give money to the little children, especially the AIDS and crack babies, so they could get treatment." The neighborhood where Jasmine lives is not a safe one, so she doesn't play outside there. "Daddy says there's too many drug dealers and they shoot a lot," she says. But in the pictures she draws, such as her award-winning contest entry, her images are almost always rainbows, flowers, parks, and sunshine. "A lot of people look for excuses for why they can't succeed," says Mr. Jaffe, Jasmine's art teacher. "Then you have a child like Jasmine, who has every reason to fail and yet is successful far above everyone's expectations."

My neighborhood is like a hell hole. All you see are people selling drugs and doing drugs, too. I don't feel right when I see them doing that. Because that makes me say to my self "hey"! I hope I don't do that stuff. But I say to my self "they can't make me do that because I'm strong and I can say "NO".

My Neighborhood needs work done on it because there are too many vacant lots around here. I'll bet that who ever is reading my letter is scared to send their child to the store! If you are, I know what it feels like. There are two around my building. Sometimes I am afraid to go to the garbage. Sometimes I cry because I want to move where there's nothing bad. But every where I have moved there are some people doing something bad.

I hope you liked it ☺

ALEXANDER BROOKS - AGE 12

THE WALLS OF ALEXANDER BROOKS'S ROOM ARE lined with his drawings - cartoons, landscapes, and portraits. Alex wants to be an artist or an architect when he grows up. His mother says he's talented with his hands. She displays a boat he carved out of a piece of wood he found, and says he even fixed her vacuum cleaner. "He's a good Christian young man," she says. "I'm proud of him. He's got expectations. He's going somewhere." Alex also writes poetry and sings in church. His art teacher, Mr. Jaffe, says that Alex and his three brothers are extremely talented in the arts - talent, he suggests, that was developed and encouraged by their artistic mother. "Alex is easily on a high school level," he says, "maybe even college. I could put some of his pieces in a portfolio and get him into the Art Institute school."

ALEXANDER BROOKS

When asked about the drawing he did for the "My Neighborhood" contest, Alex says he got the idea for his winning entry when he was outside, sitting on a hill with his friends. "I thought how it would be to fly like a bird, and how things would look from above, and that's how I drew that picture." On the back of Alex's entry he wrote a note to himself, "Don't forget to take me to school. Don't let Mr. Jaffe down."

LIVING ONE DAY AT A TIME

My neighborhood is like a scenery of a make-believe land. I live in the Washington Park Projects. My mother and I have not lived here a year. Since we have been living here, I've found that where ever you live, life has its ups and downs. I have also found that you really have to be strong. There is always a series of break-ins, murders outside of the building, constant shooting, police cars coming to lock someone up, fire trucks passing to put out fires, children and adults getting hit by cars while trying to cross the streets or trying to catch the bus. Leaving for school is scary. You never know when you might get shot. You never know when someone might shoot at you out of a window. We have a lot of vacant lots and abandoned buildings in our neighborhood.

There is no one trying to help the community. Sometimes I feel trapped within my home. My mother worries about my safety, just as I worry about hers. My mother is very strong and she keeps me strong. She pushes me very hard to do better and achieve my goals. She always tells me, "Be who you want to be in life and don't give up!" I feel as though the world and the people may come to an end. There is too much violence and black on black crime within our city and around the world. No one seems to care about the children of the future.

MORRELL McCLINTON - AGE 13

Living in Cabrini Green

The housing project called Cabrini Green
Where people get shot over silly things
In my book it's called killing town
People get killed just for walking around
It's like a massacre that will not stop
Black on Black killing all around the clock
It's hurt's my heart so bad can't you see
Black people getting killed everyday on the street
Now back to the story and here it goes
A little boy got shot and straight hit the floor
His mother jumped to the ground with no thought in
her head
She already knew that her baby was dead
She screamed and screamed as loud as she could
Her son was another person who got killed in the hood

PRINCE RAGGS - AGE 14

She looked around to see where it came from

A man on the roof with a sawed off shot gun

The way he got shot it was oh so cold

He was in the first grade. Only seven years old.

He didn't even make it out of grammar school

Because of somedum trigger happy fool.

In his class he was doing very fine

He was just in the wrong place at the wrong time

The police came and the news did too

His mother was so scared she didn't know what to do

The memories of her son drifted in her head

She thinking of the time she used to tuck him in bed

No more of that because he's long gone

But his mother know that she ain't alone

Two other kid's got killed the very same year

Leaving there parents eyes with bunch of tears

PRINCE DOESN'T LIVE IN CABRINI GREEN. HE LIVES IN A PROJECT IN another part of the city. It didn't matter to Prince that he was supposed to write about *his* neighborhood for the contest. What mattered to him was that a little boy had just been killed, and he needed to write about it.

Prince doesn't talk much. He gets his point across by writing with passion and intelligence about the things he sees and feels. The principal of his school, Mr. Hall, says Prince is always writing and will frequently bring his work to the office to show him. Prince says of his writing, "It's just in my head, and I write it down." As one of his school's academic achievers, Prince is involved in the University of Illinois at Chicago Scholars Program. He also has been a frequent representative for his school at district academic events. This summer he will work with children at UIC.

Tall, good-looking, smart and athletic, Prince is just the type of kid gangs look for, and he has had to fight to stay out of them. As the warm weather brings recruiting time, Prince's focus remains on what is important to him: school and sports - basketball, boxing, and long-distance running. At home, Prince helps care for three brothers and a 4-year-old sister. He says he'd like to make the world a better place. "If I had my way," he says, "I would change the world around. I'd help the homeless people and wouldn't make it so hard for them to make something of themselves."

PRINCE RAGGS

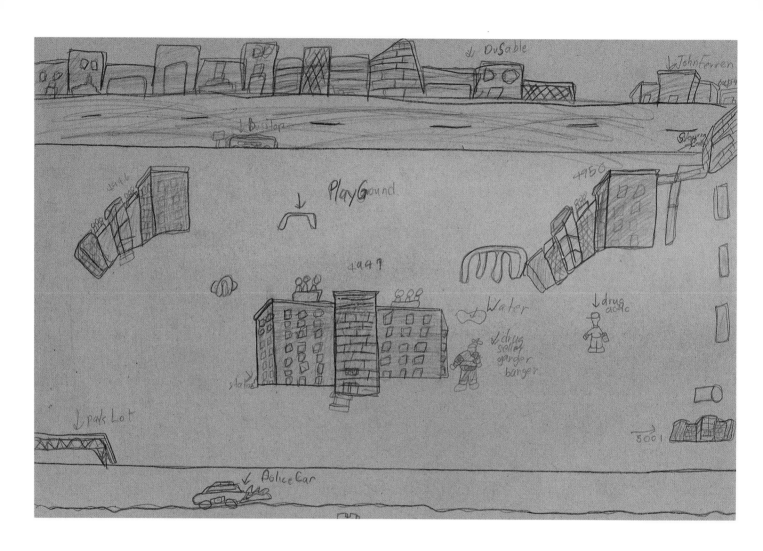

JOHNTA GATSON · AGE 10

57

My place and life

Hello my name is Charlie Williams as you might know I live in a slum some people call it a hell on earth and so do I. My neighborhood is not a nice place we have rats, roches, spiders, and killers. some not with guns but with drugs I love my family I spend most of my time at home in the house I don't want to be one lesser black male dead. I pha to be a doctor after 8 years in collage if I don't get caught up in gangs or girls. I want to have a couple of kids one boy and one girl a wife a big house and one dog. My neighborhood is so bad that if you gave any fool a gun with no bullets he will try his best to shoot it. people say my area is the worst place on earth but I'm surviving. I have a roof over my head a bed to sleep on a tv of my own and a nice family.

JAMAL MORRIS - AGE 11

My name is Omeka Mitchell.
I live in a bad project. The name of it
the 4120 Building. It's called high
rise. Our Neighborhood is very loud at.
Night. The only time it is quite is about
One o'clock in the Morning. We can hear
all the shoting and mothers crying.
most of the night. Parents are Scared
for their children to leave the building.
Most Parents are scared for their Children
to wear name brand, clothes and Shoes,
because of the Violence. It can cause.
Most children are afraid to walk
down a Calument street.
      What can we do to
Stop the Violence? Some people
don't think there's any future for
Children. My mom told me. that she
does want anything to happen
to me. So we I come home
from School The only things that
I can do are go to the store
and play in the playground. I
wish someone would stop and
Stop the Violence.

POLICE

John Fiske School

My neighborhood is filled with both good and bad and some of these things really make me mad, When Children are neglected and running all around when bottles, cans and broken glass are lying on the ground.

Besides all the bad things in my neighborhood, I overcome the thought of them by thinking of the good. Starting with the nice people that I see each day, and the little children who love to run and play, my neighborhood is often played like a game I ike the good things and hope they stay the same

CHEYNEY WORTHAM - AGE 12

WALLACE MARSHALL - AGE 12
64

PATRICK CLEMONS - AGE 14

65

WHAT I SEE

AS I LOOK AROUND WHAT DO I SEE?

A BIRD, SOME GRASS, A TREE.

SOME TALL RED AND WHITE BUILDINGS JUTTING UP TO THE SKY,

MAKING EVERTTHING LOOK SO SMALL BECAUSE THEY ARE SO HIGH.

SOME DRUGDEALERS TRYING TO MAKE A DEAL,

HUNGRY PEOPLE STANDING ON THE CORNER BEGGING FOR A MEAL.

IT'S SAD WHEN YOU COME TO THINK OF IT,

BUT MOST PEOPLE DON'T CARE-NOT EVEN A LITTLE BIT.

ALL THE GANGBANGERS ARE KNOWN AROUND HERE,

FOR SMOKING MARIJUANA OR TURNING UP A CAN OF BEER.

I KNOW IT'S SAD TO SAY,

BUT THE SAME THINGS GO ON EACH AND EVERYDAY.

THIS IS EXACTLY WHAT I SEE.

I HOPE THIS NEIGHBORHOOD WILL CHANGE FOR EVERYONE NOT JUST FOR ME.

SANDRA PORTER - AGE 12

Omar Lewis - Age 12

RONNIE CHANDLER - AGE 10

69

The Projects

The Projects the Projects they have cops,
The Projects the Projects where people sell rocks
The Projects the Projects where we have bugs,
The Projets the Projects where we have thugs,
The Projects the Projects where people kill in the night
The Projects the Projects where people get hype.
So here's my poem of the projects,
Don't move here because of the wrecks.

The Projects the Projects where they shot me,
The Projects the Projects have B.D.'s and G.D.'s.
The Projects the Projects we have murders,
The Projects the Projects we hear killings
The Projects the Projects we don't have rugs
The Projects the Projects we have drugs.
The Projects are not a good place to live
but I'm thankful I have a roof.
Some people don't have a roof and die
so I'm gonna be very thankful.
Peace to the middle east my brother. and
mother

CHRISTOPHER UPSHAW - AGE 11

CHRIS IS ANGRY. HE'S ANGRY ABOUT THE projects, and the gangs, and the drugs. "These projects need to be fixed up. Look at 'em. They're all messed up, with their gangsters - their B.D.'s and G.D.'s (Black Disciples and Gangster Disciples) - and their finger signs and handshakes. People doin' drugs and beatin' up on babies. It don't make no sense," he says.

An intelligent boy, Chris earns mostly A's and B's in school. He says his favorite classes are math and reading. "You should see my desk," he says. "Ain't nothing but newspapers, magazines, and books." Chris has been in the 99th percentile in his school, although this past year he slipped a little. This seems to coincide with some changes in his living arrangements. He is currently living with his grandmother in the Robert Taylor Homes. When asked about his mother he replies, "I don't know where my mother's at." The oldest of the three brothers living together, Chris also has a brother in a foster home and a brother and sister who live elsewhere. He says his grandmother talks about taking them to live in the country, but he would like to live nearby with his dad.

Photo by Patricia Evans

CHRISTOPHER UPSHAW

Whatever Chris is doing, he can't seem to escape the violence of the projects, and he can't seem to stop talking about it. "I don't know why they invented guns," he says. "I could see knives, 'cause it's useful for other stuff, not just for killing people. Ain't no sense just to go around shooting somebody 'cause they in the wrong place at the wrong time." Chris has an uncle who was shot in the leg.

Sometimes when talking about the projects, Chris shakes his head and even laughs at how crazy it all seems. It is not a good-natured laugh. It is an angry one. He describes a woman who was high on drugs and threw her baby down the garbage chute because it wouldn't stop crying. And he talks about men who feed infants cocaine to get them hooked. He admits that there are people who may not like his poem about the projects, but says, "If they come around here and live here as long as I have, they be saying the same things. They wouldn't want to live here for a minute." Chris says he plans to go to college and would like to study business and law. Then he'd like to run for judge and put away all the gangbangers. He has no plans to become part of a gang. "I ain't been in no gang, and I ain't gonna get in no gang," he says. "What goes around comes around. And it's comin' around."

In my neighborhood
it's kind of bad.
It has vacant buildings.
Alleys.
Lots of houses, trees, and fields
Bushes
Words on buildings
Grounds,

gangs.

Standing in front of my buildings
Seeing people talking,,

running, playing, fighting

Dying.

Needs to stop

Needs to put building in vacant fields

Needs to do something with the alleys.

Just do something for the future.

Protect ourselves

Go to school

Life

Hope

We can.

THE FOCUS OF SYNOBIA'S LIFE IS her church. Every day after school she goes to services and meetings, and often takes care of the small children while their parents are worshipping. "People love and respect me there," she says.

Synobia entered the contest because people say she is a good writer. Synobia often writes poetry and worked on her award-winning entry for four days, revising it until she had it just right. She says she wants to use the $250 prize money for college. She'd like to go to the University of Chicago, and is now working on getting her grade point level high enough to go to Hyde Park High School. "I'm gonna do it," she says confidently, "because I do all my work."

SYNOBIA DAWKINS

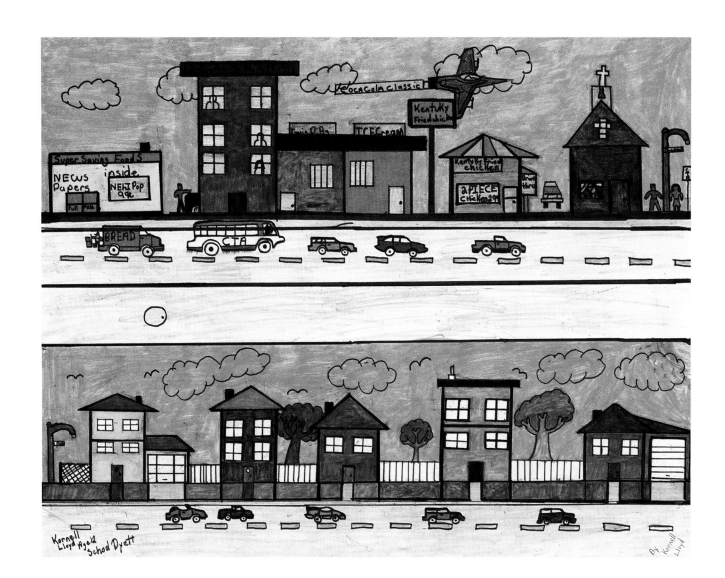

KORNELL LLOYD - AGE 12

LESTER BOMMEN - AGE 12

My neighborhood is so bad,
It makes you sad!
It's not fun, because they have guns
Don't go outside to get a rider,
Because they might skin your hide,
Don't go out singing, for you might get
Stopped If not, you might get popped.
Don't hang out in the neighborhood
Because that is understood
I'm telling you the truth, it is bad!
Things that will ring might get you
in trouble
So don't be a fool, stay in school
and do your work
Don't be a jerk,

They look like trashy with their masks
They don't care, and it's very unfair.
Keep the project clean.
Do you know what I mean?
Now they are crying
Because their freinds are dying.
Don't do drugs
For they'll carry you away wrapped in a rug.
There are drugs and they make you
act like silly bugs.
Don't start crying, when you
start dying, because
you know you were using
drugs.

NICOLE LAMPKINS · AGE 10

JOANNE MILLER - AGE 14

ALTHOUGH JOANNE'S ART TEACHER PRAISES HER AS AN outstanding student, Joanne herself is reluctant to talk about her abilities. She says she enjoys her art classes, but she also likes to read and sing and "hang out" with her friends and her four sisters.

What Joanne speaks vehemently about is the violence, and how it affects the children. "We need to talk to the younger kids about the people in the street, but all that talking hardly does anything for them," she says. She describes a lecture she went to on drug abuse. "I thought it would be boring," she says, "but they told us a lot of things - like how drugs affect your body. Younger kids need to hear this. They don't seem to care. If one of them's gone - it's just another person gone. Most of the time I'm thinking that's sad."

Joanne is concerned that if people don't intervene, the children will be lost. "If they don't help young kids, they're just gonna end up killing each other," she says. "And all the stuff they're killing each other for just ain't worth it."

JOANNE MILLER (RIGHT)

Your neighborhood is so neat that you can walk around it in peace and not get jumped on. You don't see shooting around little children or giving the little kids any drugs. Every where you go. you probably see nice flowers or you see nice things in people's back yards. You see plants and other things.

But if you came to my neighborhood you will meet a lot of gangbangers and you will end up joining them. When you go around the neighborhood you will see young members. Then again, sometimes you won't. But the reason I am writing this neighborhood story is so you can learn a little about me. I am a good person and I don't bother any one.

I wish my neighborhood could be a nice place to be where you won't get bothered with. I wish it could be clean, no garbage around where you would see nice People and you'll see people walking dogs. You'll see nice trees and nice grass, little kids, and nice animals. That's what makes the neighborhood soso good. It will be so nice that you might want to live there. so, when the people come around this neighborhood they'll see nice grass they will see play grounds, swimming pools and gym rooms and lots of more activites, we'll have baseball teams and football teams. When you go in a neighbor's house you would see cable tv floor-model. You would even see a nice yard full of things. People would

JAMES FREEMAN - AGE 14

83

have a table and chairs sitting in the back yard. Some would have swimming pools. They would have basements so that when It gets cold out side and you don't want to bring your dog in the house, he can go in the basement. Also, a basement is for when you want to wash your clothes you can have your clothes in the basement with the washing machine and dryers.

My dream neighborhood would not have all that fighting or shooting at one another. Where as, if you go around the Stateway gardens housing projects you might get shot or killed. That's what makes the neighborhood so special, in a negative way. One of these days I hope to live in that dream neighborhood.

TRACY WILLIAMS - AGE 14
8 5

My neighborhood is good in some places and bad in some places. Where I live now they shoot sometimes and kills sometimes. I would like to go where it is peace.

I will like to go where it is no shooting, killing or stealing or fighting. I hope this city could be a better place before the gangs take over the neighborhood.

The police need more help so they can go and look where they think they might find guns and other weapons. We need to come together black and white and fight together against crime.

We need peace in our country. And we need a good mayor, a good president and better schools, better houses. We need to change the streets and alleys. We need to help homeless people get a place to stay. I hope this city becomes a better place for every one, not one color, all colors.

CHRISTOPHER EUBANKS · AGE 13

"**P**EACE," SAYS CHRISTOPHER, "IS IN THE country." Momence, an area south of the city, is where Christopher finds peace. He has been there three times. There, he says, "you could sleep outside, you could leave the door open, you could leave stuff outside. You leave anything outside around here, somebody steal it." Around where Christopher lives, he finds little peace. "They always shoot at each other," he says. "They be living together, across the street from each other and they be shooting at each other." He says he has a brother who was shot by the gangs. "I used to get down when there's shooting, but now I'm used to it. I just get away from the window."

A good student in school, Christopher is in the University of Illinois Scholars Program, and enjoys the trips they take to the university and other schools. Christopher also likes to play the drums, but sports is his favorite pastime. He collects baseball cards and plays softball and football.

At home, Christopher, the fifth oldest of nine children, helps his mother with the cooking and cleaning, and he helps his younger brothers and sister with their homework. He'd like to see the world change. "I'd like to get the homeless people off the street and send them back to school so they could get jobs," he says. "And I'd clean up the neighborhood and get rid of the guns and drugs. We need to help people out."

CHRISTOPHER EUBANKS

88

In my neighborhood all races live together, In my neighborhood drugs dont belong,

In my neighborhood evil is but a song, then when i get home after school,

which to me is an important tool, on the end of the block their i stand,

looking at something grand, something that i hold dear, and only i could,

to look and stare at my neighborhood, in my neighborhood the buildings stand tall,

and in the trees sweet birds call, IN my neighborhood no things fight,

and in my neighborhood kids can fly their kites, but there is something i wish,

not to speak, something in my heart I hold deep, two places which stays apart,

two places which do have hearts, two places which one day will come together,

with love and dignity, hope and devotion, this will be called the peace notion,

MY neighborhood might not be the best , but i wouldnt give it up for anything LESS.

JOSEPH HARRIS · AGE 13

When I look out on my neighborhood, I see lots of spaces to build things like video stores, pizza places, and playgrounds with treehouses. There are schools and churches and a library. There is lots of space for bike riding on the bike trail. I can even see the Museum of Science and Industry near me. I'm right off the Lake Michigan, so if I go a little further, I will be at the beach where I go swimming. I see buildings that need to be torn down that now have lots of drug activities. I see garbage that needs to be picked up.

At first, I moved to my house and thought that it was a wreck because it was very dirty , and there were a lot of insects. The house had almost no light. It needed a lot of construction and electrical work for the development of the house. I could have been eaten up or bitten because the lady next door had two big dogs, and the fence had fallen down. Now it is fixed up. It has changed and there are improvements. In the front, we have a bush and lots of flowers. The backyard has a very large space and it can be used for a parking lot. The people next door said that they like our house now and so they wanted to fix up their house, so they did. The next day, the lady on the next block complimented us on the hard work that we did to our house.

Now what makes up a good neighborhood is good people who are good neighbors. They will do kind things for each other. If you have a relationship with your neighbors, you can invite them to a Halloween party and a Thanksgiving party. You can baby sit if the parents are not home. If you see a suspicious character, you can call 911 for the police. Good neighbors are people who care.

Here is my recipe for a good neighborhood:

3 cups of a clean neighborhood

4 cups of good people

1/4 cup of love

Put it in the pot of obedience of the law

beat it and put it in the oven of goodwill

Turn it on high and leave it in for 20 minutes.

Take it out and that's your neighborhood.

KHARI'S RECIPE MIGHT BE WHIMSICAL, BUT when Khari speaks he is serious and intense. It's as if there is a war-weary man inside this small boy's body. He cannot seem to take his mind away from the violence, and he talks about it incessantly. "You can see people killing and killing and drugs," he says. "You see needles. You see it on TV. This is not a world you want to be in. You see people on the streets. You see them dying. The world in the 90's is not what it should be. Killing is not the solution. All they're doing is taking another life."

Khari feels it's important that people listen to him, "even," he says, "if sometimes I can be boring." He thinks that if people listen they may learn something. "You can get a little insight - just a little bit of a better insight on what you should be working on every day to make the world better," he says. "That's what my recipe was for. Even though you can't do it for real, you should follow it every day to make your life better and society's life better."

Khari is not sure what he'd like to be - maybe a scientist, or an astronaut, or a civil rights leader, or a preacher. For now, he's concentrating on surviving. "All the kids are getting hurt and I'm the only one surviving," he says. "I stay away from drugs. My family respects me for that, 'cause I'm thinking to stay alive."

KHARI WOOLFOLK

9 3

The perfect nieghborhood

Take out all the drugs put in plenty of hugs. Take out all the ganges put in the other good thangs and do you have a perfect neirborhood were every one wants to live but you well have to give something to get somthing good out of. This neiborhood which is like a bright light that sticks out in the city.

KEINEH WHITLEY - AGE 12

My Life in Stateway

Here come the police to fight all the crime and dope.

The people in Stateway have given up hope.

To stay in my neighborhood you have to be bad.

If you don't fight back you are not going to last.

For there are some good people in

Stateway for this is true you can
count them on your hands for there
are a few.

"Oh Stateway, Oh Stateway I know
you could do better but I guess us
few good people just don't matter.

As I sit in my room and look at
the crime below, I think to myself
where is a 12-year-old to go

Oh Stateway, Oh Stateway, I know your hands
are full of fighting all the crime and dope. But
give us few good people a sign of hope.

ZENOVIA TREADWELL · AGE 12

ZENOVIA KNOWS TWO MEANINGS OF THE WORD "bad;" the traditional meaning, and the kind of bad that means you fight back. "If you grow up here," she says, "you grow up strong enough to say no. If somebody want to get you in a gang, you be bad enough to say no and get away."

Zenovia believes the gangs are what caused the people in her projects to give up hope. "At first, everyone was doing everything right. After the gangs came, people didn't stop 'em. They just gave up." She says the gangs fight over dope, but, "if you take away the dope, they still be fighting over guns - who's got the bigger guns."

If Zenovia had her way, she would get out of the neighborhood. She says her family is looking for a nicer place to live. When asked where a

ZENOVIA TREADWELL

nicer place is, she answers, "Where the white kids live is the nicer places." She wants to live where she's not afraid someone is going to start shooting. "You never know when they're gonna start," she says. "I see them on the playground, in front of the building, behind the tree."

Zenovia escapes the violence of her neighborhood by going out with her two brothers. Close in age (the brothers are 14 and 11), the three visit the stores and the movies in Oak Park, a nearby suburb. As the only girl in the family, Zenovia also enjoys the shopping trips she takes with her mother. A good student, Zenovia is in the University of Illinois Scholars Program at school. With a sense of pride softened by a sweet smile, Zenovia admits that she's smart, then adds, "and I have a lot of potential."

My neighborhood is not the most beautiful place in the world
neither is it the healthiest environment for children to grow
up in , but in my eyes there is some beauty to be found.
Beauty such as the few parks where the children play and the
lake that is nearby. There are many trees big and beautiful ,
the grass , and the birds. These Beauties are simple but true
and their in my neighborhood.

All of these things are fine but very few. They are few because
there is so much of other things negative things. Things like
drugs , the dealers , the gangs , guns and death.

I look out of my window and see drugs being sold or someone
being shot. I want to freeze time and prevent it from happening
but I know time waits for no one. The street dwellers say things
like " I'm only doing this to make a little extra money or just
for a little while." But what they fail to realize that the money
comes so fast they instinctively know they can't stop.
It's the same with drug attics , they can't stop until they die
or end up in jail. Sadly enough , that is the only out come for
the street dwellers.

All that time and energy is just wasted. Many of them should be
in school , and many are parents who should be setting better
examples for their children. Many of them have great minds all
going to waste. I hope the children of today will make this
world a better place for the children of tomorrow.

PAULETTE HYNEMAN AGE 12

WILLIAM FORD - AGE 13

103

We need TO ALL Join Hands to Build a better neighborhood

MEMBERS OF TAKEESHA'S FAMILY SAY SHE'S THE TYPE OF PERSON you can ask to do anything, and she'll do it. Living together in a three-story brick house, Takeesha's extended family spans four generations and includes 12 children ranging in age from 8 months to 15 years. For the occasion of Takeesha's photograph, everyone gathered on the front stoop, and the session quickly took on the feeling of a family party. One of six siblings, Takeesha is the oldest girl, and helps take care of the younger ones.

The inspiration for Takeesha's drawing came from her feeling that people need to pull together, and that they need to work with each other to make the neighborhood better. "They need to build more playgrounds, give more people jobs," she says. "And people need to stop being around shooting."

An honor roll student in school, Takeesha has won awards for achievement and attendance. She likes music, skating, and going to the movies. "I would like to be a doctor," she says, "because I like helping people get better."

TAKEESHA LITTLE (CENTER) AND FAMILY

"My Neighborhood" Contest Winners

Afterword
BY JAMES P. COMER, M.D.
Maurice Falk Professor of Child Psychiatry
Yale Child Study Center

● ● ●

OVER THE YEARS I HAVE RECEIVED THOUSANDS OF LETTERS FROM CHILDREN. Many of these young people were students at the schools our programs were involved with. Others were not, and were writing because of something they'd read about me or by me. Regardless of the circumstances under which the correspondence occurred, I have always valued the opportunity to hear about children's experiences firsthand. Ours is a society that undervalues the wealth our youth have to offer, and we have paid dearly for that. Those of us who are serious about becoming better parents and educators must listen to our children.

In reading the letters and poems of children, I have been able to see the world, their world, through their eyes. I continue to be amazed at the extent to which the perspective and experiences of young people provide me with hope and direction. I see hope in the cases of young people who have been fortunate enough to take advantage of the benefits of a solid educational system, or a system that has benefitted from school reform programs, such as our School Development Program. The lives and stories of these children also provide direction. I am constantly reminded of the magnitude of the needs of these children who suffer because of the larger socio-economic issues of poverty, racism, sexism and the resulting crime and hopelessness.

In spite of the despair that many of these children face, they cling to hope for a better world. Their hope for better homes, schools, and neighborhoods is our responsibility. That is why *My Neighborhood* is so important. It provides all of us with an opportunity to hear from children in the inner city. These children - our children - are our responsibility. Their words not only remind us of that responsibility, but provide us with direction to act on their behalf.

My Neighborhood is far more than a moving collection of personal essays. It is an opportunity for educators, parents and children across the nation to look at the American inner city through the eyes of its youth. These essays, poems and pictures are unforgettable, both because of the images they portray, and the voices behind those images. Every teacher should read this book.

About the Schools

• • •

THROUGH OUR INVOLVEMENT IN THE "M**Y** N**EIGHBORHOOD**" PROJECT, WE HAD THE OPPORTUNITY TO VISIT ALMOST 20 PARTICIPATING ELEMENTARY SCHOOLS. Much of what we saw there impressed us and contradicted the chaotic conditions we had expected. Although the school system is fraught with problems and deficiencies, there are a number of dedicated teachers and principals who are striving to give their students the nurturing, education, and guidance they need, frequently with little or no support from parents or government agencies. We felt they were an important part of the "My Neighborhood" story. Ignoring the odds and statistics, many of these educators instruct their students as if they are all candidates for higher education. This instruction must often go well beyond the traditional bounds of education. Teachers take on the roles of mothers and fathers by offering students the discipline and support lacking in some of their home lives. The schools themselves provide such basics as shelter and balanced meals to children who might not get them anywhere else.

The schools share much in common in general academics and programs. Computer labs, remedial classes, and special counseling are standard. A number of schools have also adopted an African/African-American centered curriculum in which the basics are taught through the African/African-American perspective. After-school programs play an important role in the inner city, not only for the additional learning opportunities they provide, but also for the intervention they offer through drug and substance abuse counseling, self-esteem, and social responsibility programs. These approaches frequently involve one-on-one mentoring, with teachers functioning as positive role models for children at risk. After-school programs serve another important function: they are a place for the children to be that is supervised and relatively safe. Some school principals would like to see school hours extended just for this purpose.

On an individual level, many of the schools respond to the special needs of the students with their own unique focus and programs. At the Benjamin W. Raymond School, the emphasis is on personal attention. As Principal Louis Hall walks the corridors, he is greeted with affectionate thumbs-up signs, handshakes, and hugs. The approachable Mr. Hall says that Raymond's philosophy is that all children can learn—irrespective of their background or impairments. This is evidenced by the many "pull-out" and one-on-one programs Raymond offers to kids at risk. For advanced students, two new urban education programs affiliated with Illinois Institute of Technology and the Scholars Program at the University of Illinois at Chicago, provide additional encouragement and opportunities to learn. Individual attention is so important at Raymond that a school official is sent to visit the home of a student who has been absent for more than two days.

The Helen J. McCorkle School uses an art-centered curriculum to motivate students. The school's staff believes that this curriculum which focuses on and integrates all subjects with the arts, will contribute to greater student appreciation of the aesthetic as well as practical values of what they learn. The arts are also used to develop motor skills and positive self-image.

The unique personality of the Carter G. Woodson South School is defined by an abundance of school and individual pride. Cheerleaders, monthly school spirit days, and Woodson South sweatshirts, all encourage this sense of pride. On the "Someone You Should Know" bulletin board, names of students share the spotlight with names of famous African Americans. In the first grade classroom, there is an "Author's Chair" in which one student per day has the honor of sitting and reading his or her original work.

Commerce is flourishing at the Ludwig von Beethoven School. Every two weeks the gift shop, located in a second floor classroom, is open for business. In this store, which is entirely student run, students, parents, teachers, and shoppers looking for bargains, can purchase a range of trinkets, decorative items and toys. The money that is earned is then deposited in a bank account and used to fund programs for the school. With an emphasis on practical learning, Beethoven School has frequently been at the forefront of initiating motivational programs for students, parents, and community residents. The Beethoven Project, started several years ago, is a pilot program offering young mothers-to-be training and counseling in prenatal care.

The William J. and Charles H. Mayo School has the distinction of having the first elementary school marching band and ballet troupe ever to perform at Walt Disney World. Both the band and the ballet company have enjoyed national honors. In academics, Mayo's "Young Authors" program offers students a special way to exhibit their talents through writing and illustrating original stories. These highly imaginative and beautifully bound works are then entered into competitions. Mayo has had several local and citywide winners.

Students at the Florence B. Price school have a variety of options through which to find motivation. Price itself uses a thematic, hands-on approach to cooperative learning. The curriculum this past year was set up around the themes of Africa, India, Japan and Mexico. The Foundations at Price, a school-within-a-school, offers a whole language holistic approach to learning. But the shining star of the school is the piano lab—a pilot program designed to teach children reading, writing, numbers and coordination through music. This seems appropriate since Price is named after an early 20th-century African-American woman who was a distinguished pianist and composer.

There are many other school programs that deserve recognition, not because they are unique in the realm of education, but because they are unique in the communities in which they exist, and because they contradict the stereotype of inner-city schools. They are also critical to the children, who have few other opportunities to find motivation, instruction, and supervision. There has been much discussion about the failures of Chicago's school system. As children pass from elementary to high school, they find their academic needs are not being met. Inner-city high school graduation rates average about 50%, with Martin Luther King Jr. High School at 29% and others as low as 17%.* Violence, inferior academic motivation, and sub-standard facilities are well-documented. That's why it is so important to recognize and encourage the people and the programs that are succeeding. They are the best chance the system has to hold on to the kids.

Just as we need to make the neighborhoods better for the children, we need to make the schools better by demanding responsible, supportive action. Without such action, the wonderful potential exhibited by the children might be lost forever. That is a loss we cannot afford.

*School year 1991-92. Source: Chicago Board of Education

About the "My Neighborhood" Project

• • •

THE "MY NEIGHBORHOOD" CONTEST WAS SPONSORED BY HYDE PARK BANK, A COMMUNITY BANK LOCATED ON CHICAGO'S MID-SOUTH SIDE. THE contest began on October 5, 1992 and ended on November 6, 1992. Eligibility was open to students between the ages of 5 and 14 who attend elementary schools in five south side communities around the bank. The contest invited children to describe their neighborhoods in words or pictures. First, second, and third place prizes were awarded in each of four categories: Pictures - ages 5 to 9; pictures - ages 10 to 14; words - ages 5 to 9; and words - ages 10 to 14. There were two special merit prizes and one best-of-show. In addition, 17 students received honorable mentions. First place and special merit prize winners received $500 U.S. Savings Bonds, second place received $250 bonds, third place received $100 bonds, and honorable mentions received $50 bonds. The school of the best-of-show winner received a $1000 cash prize. Eight other schools were awarded $200 cash prizes for their high level of participation, and two schools were given $500 cash for their extraordinary efforts.

Every student who entered the contest received a "My Neighborhood" certificate of merit and a book bag with the slogan, "I'm a winner in my neighborhood."

Over 600 students entered the contest. Since we could not include all the entries in the book, we tried to select those we felt best represented and expressed the thoughts and feelings of the majority. All of the entries in the book have been reproduced in their original form, as the students submitted them.

All proceeds from the *My Neighborhood* book will go to the Hyde Park Bank Foundation. This not-for-profit organization, maintained by Hyde Park Bank, sponsors programs for the schools and children in the communities surrounding the bank. The Foundation is supported by donations from Hyde Park Bank, individuals, foundations, and corporations.

About the Author

• • •

Linda Waldman is president and creative director of Waldman & Associates, Inc, the marketing agency that conceived and organized the "My Neighborhood" project for Hyde Park Bank. She attended the University of Wisconsin and Northwestern University and currently resides in Chicago.

Acknowledgements

● ● ●

THERE IS AN AFRICAN SAYING THAT, "IT TAKES AN ENTIRE VILLAGE TO RAISE ONE CHILD." The same theory could be applied to the "My Neighborhood" project. Coordinating the "My Neighborhood" contest and publishing this book could not have been possible without the help, guidance, and nurturing of many.

From the beginning, the project has been generously and consistently fostered by Hyde Park Bank. Executives of the bank devoted their resources, financial support, and personal time. From the sponsorship of the "My Neighborhood" contest, to the publication of this book, and the development of neighborhood programs through the Hyde Park Bank Foundation, the bank has unwaveringly exhibited its dedication to the children and the community.

Without the commitment of bank president Timothy Goodsell, the "My Neighborhood" contest which gave the children a voice, and the subsequent book which carried that voice forth, would never have been possible. Other bank executives who contributed their time and energy were Patrick Barrett, Jay Fahn and Georgene Pavelec.

Two others deserve particular credit: Mitchell McNeil, who designed Hyde Park Bank's brochure and this book, and who lent his art direction to every phase of the project; and Nancy Drew, who painstakingly and insightfully edited *My Neighborhood*.

There are many others whose participation has been invaluable: Alex Kotlowitz for his advice; Jacqueline Heard of the *Chicago Tribune*, who was the first person in the press to realize the value of the children's words and pictures; Bill Harris for his wise counsel and the Harris Foundation for its generous donation; Deborah Leff for her personal support and the commitment of the Joyce Foundation; the LaSalle Bank Foundation, Chicago Title and Trust and Ariel Capital Management for their donations; Arne Duncan for his efforts on our behalf; Dr. James Comer for his eloquent afterword; Lisa Genesen for her compelling photography; Gordana Trbuhovich, who helped administer the contest; Lt. Richard Shinners of the Chicago Police 21st District, who along with Sgts. Louis Frazer, John Gallivan, and John Hardy went above and beyond the call of duty; the teachers and principals of the elementary schools for granting our many requests; and the parents and families of the children who so graciously welcomed us into their homes.

Most of all we value the children for their honesty, their eloquence, and their courage. We could not include every contest entry in the book, but we hope the ones we selected will speak for all of the children. Their voices are an inspiration, and it is a privilege to know them. They are all winners.

Linda Waldman

Index of Student Names

• • •